a product of
CHRIST

DISCOVER JESUS AND HIS
TRANSFORMING POWER SIMPLY

a product of
CHRIST

ANNA SCHULTZ AND HEATHER HENDON

Carpenter's Son Publishing

A PRODUCT OF CHRIST

Published by Carpenter's Son Publishing,

Franklin, Tennessee

Published in association with Larry Carpenter of Christian Book Services, LLC

www.christianbookservices.com

Unless otherwise indicated, Scripture quotations are from
The Holy Bible, New King James Version (NKJV)
©1982 by Thomas Nelson, Inc. Used by permission. All rights reserved.

Other Scripture quotations are from *The Amplified Bible,* Classic Edition (AMPC)
©1954, 1958, 1962, 1964, 1965, 1987 by the Lockman Foundation.

Cover Design by Suzanne Lawing

Edited by Thomas Womack

Interior Design and Proofread by Adept Content Solutions

Printed in the United States of America

978-1-949572-59-9

ACKNOWLEDGMENTS

We want to first acknowledge and thank our heavenly Father for choosing us to write this book. To our husbands, thank you for your love and patience throughout this process. Without your help, we couldn't have spent the countless hours on the phone and in prayer. Thank you to the past and present leadership at Crosspoint Fellowship and Springhill Christian Center for the lasting impact you've made on our lives. To our editor, Thomas Womack, thank you for your insight and for enduring the postal system on our behalf. To our publisher, Larry, thank you for helping us bring this vision to light.

To our dads, Jack and Mark.

Thank you for the countless prayers.

*We wouldn't be where we are
today without them.*

*Most of all, thank You to our
heavenly Father for answering them.*

CONTENTS

PREFACE

This book is intended for the recently saved or for those who want more of Jesus. It's not meant to replace the infallible Word of God, the Bible. The Bible is the ultimate authority; it exceeds all things. No person, figure, or book—including this one—is superior to the Word of the living God.

The modern church is asleep and needs an awakening. Christians are no longer discernable from unbelievers. These "Christians" are nothing like Christ. They go to church on Sundays but live a sinful life. When we sin, we're actually sinning against God. Though you may fall to temptation, you cannot habitually practice sin. There's nothing that God won't forgive you for if you earnestly seek Him and repent. The true gospel has been replaced by a feel-good message, and those who don't know Christ aren't complaining.

We've seen firsthand the lack of knowledge among God's people. If those who claim to be Christians don't know Jesus, what hope is there for the rest of the world? It's easy to believe that Jesus walked the earth two thousand years ago, but why is it so hard to believe He's coming back? We have work to do, and we need to get ready. Jesus desires true disciples, not Christians in name only. Do you truly know Jesus?

If you seek Jesus, you will find Him. "Nor is there salvation in any other, for there is no other name under heaven given among men by which we must be saved" (Acts 4:12).

God will mold you into who He wants you to be if you'll only let Him. He sees who you'll become through Him, not who you've been. Becoming a product of Christ is a transformation within you that takes place one day at a time. He'll fill your every void and complete you. Scripture tells us that Saul of Tarsus was blinded for three days, and spent that time in constant prayer. He then regained his sight and spent a few days with the disciples afterward. In one week's time, he went from being an enemy of the gospel to preaching

"If you seek Jesus, you will find Him."

the gospel. What change can God make in you in one week?

In the fall of 2017, the Lord revealed to Heather that she and I were to write a book for God's people. He put on her heart that it would be a product of Christ. That's what this is—His product. He gets the glory for every word within these pages.

This book is meant to be a quick read that is easily understood. We have no intention to wow you with our words. We've spent countless hours in prayer to ensure that we give you the basics needed to kickstart your walk with Jesus. We pray that as you read this, the Holy Spirit gives you a supernatural understanding of it.

Everyone who calls upon His name should know Him, because to know Him is to love Him. This book is intended to guide you into a deeper relationship with your Savior.

"Jesus said to him, 'I am the way, the truth, and the life. No one comes to the Father except through Me'" (John 14:6).

1
CHRIST'S FINISHED WORK

For no other foundation can anyone lay than
that which is laid, which is Jesus Christ.

—1 Corinthians 3:11

It is time. God has waited on you patiently, but now it's time you understand who He is and what He wants to do in your life. You're created in His image and designed to fellowship with Him. Your spirit within you longs to be with Him—that's why even the lost cry out to Him in their final moments. You can try to fill the void in your life with drugs, alcohol, people, food, and experiences, but until you have a relationship with Jesus, you'll never be complete. You can be so much more than what you've been. You can be full and whole.

Whether you're aware of it or not, you need Him desperately. Your Savior wants you to know Him, not to just blindly claim Him.

Salvation is only the beginning. Imagine you're on vacation and have just arrived in your hotel room. As you look out over the beach, you sense promise in the future. But that's only the beginning; you haven't even put your feet in the water yet! You can swim, go parasailing, play in the sand. That's how salvation is. With God, there are endless possibilities of what's in store for you. Don't just stay in your hotel room.

When Jesus sacrificed His life at the cross, He did it for you. We all know that Jesus died and rose again, but if someone asked you what Jesus' death actually accomplished, would you know what to say? It's pivotal that you have genuine understanding of this question and not just a generic answer. To begin to understand Him, you have to understand what He did. He took your place on that cross so that you could have salvation (eternal life), justification (declaration of innocence, righteousness), and sanctification (freedom from sin). Because of His sacrifice, you're free from spiritual death and from having to spend eternity without Him. Because of that sacrifice, you have His righteousness and are free from the bondage of sin.

As glorious as Christ's resurrection was, His death was the most monumental event throughout history. But how did His death actually accomplish anything? Not just anyone can give their life for another and wash away sin. Only Jesus could do that.

Adam sinned, and the curse of sin is death. The ground was cursed, and all of creation was altered because of sin. Adam surrendered his authority to Satan through that mistake. Jesus was the only man besides Adam who wasn't born into sin. Because He remained sinless and didn't fall to temptation, He was able to redeem what Adam lost. Through what Christ did at Calvary, we're no longer subject to Satan's tactics

"*To begin to understand Him, you have to understand what He did.*"

and can have the same power that Jesus Himself had through His Holy Spirit.

You may have heard the phrase "born into sin" without understanding what it means. Since Adam first sinned, everyone has been born with the same sinful nature. Sin brings consequences, but to overcome them we have nothing worthy to offer our Creator. We deserve the punishment that Christ endured at the cross, but we don't have to endure it because He took our place. He took the punishment for mankind's sin.

You were born into sin, but by accepting Christ, you're born again into the kingdom of God. As born-again believers, we're no longer subject to the curse of the law of sin and death. We have eternal life. Our physical bodies may die, but our spirits live on with Him. You're not a body with a spirit; you're a spirit with a body, and your spirit will never be separated from Him. As Jesus said regarding the resurrection of believers from the dead, "Have you not read what was spoken to you by God, saying, 'I am the God of Abraham, the God of Isaac, and the God of Jacob'? God is not the God of the dead, but of the living" (Matthew 22:31-32). This life may be brief, but we have eternity to look forward to. As the psalmist testified, "I will walk before the Lord in the land of the living" (Psalm 116:9).

You're saved by His grace, through faith. Faith is not the means of salvation; His grace is. Faith is the avenue used. Scripture defines faith this way: "Now faith is the substance of things hoped for, the evidence of things not seen" (Hebrews 11:1). Faith is a requirement to come before the Lord; we must believe.

Without faith, many miracles throughout Scripture wouldn't have occurred. The Bible speaks of those "who through faith subdued kingdoms, worked righteousness, obtained promises, stopped the mouths of lions, quenched the violence of fire, escaped the edge of the sword, out of weakness were made strong, became valiant in battle, turned to flight the armies of the aliens" (Hebrews 11:33-34).

Have an unwavering trust and confidence in God. We have faith that our employer will pay us and that the bank will safeguard the money we deposit. We have faith in insurance companies, doctors, and even our spouse. We have faith. But our ultimate faith must be in the right place. With the proper placement of your faith, you'll have His grace. The foundation of your faith must be in what Christ accomplished at the cross. You must truly believe that His ultimate sacrifice accomplished all things.

The body of Christ is so concerned with reaching the lost (and rightly so, because it's what we're called to do) that we've forgotten those within the pews. How can you share Christ and do His work if you don't know Him? However, the blame isn't entirely on the church. It's up to each individual believer to seek the Lord with their whole heart. He's already seeking you—so when you seek Him, you'll find Him.

So many Christians are only on first base with God, and their lack of knowledge is keeping them from living a victorious life. God wants more for His people, and His church needs a breakthrough. We must have a solid understanding of the basic things of the kingdom of God and continue to mature spiritually. Jesus' finished work at the cross is the answer—not the works and rituals that religion requires. A spiritual warfare is raging, and we need Jesus. Don't settle when He wants you to have more of Him.

The Lord warned the children of Israel against rejecting the things of God, and this warning applies to His people (the church) today: "My people are destroyed for lack of knowledge" (Hosea 4:6). There are people who claim the Christian faith but who don't have a clue who Christ is. Don't be willingly blind.

The things of God don't have to be complicated and intimidating, as the apostle Paul made clear: "And I, brethren, when I came to you, did not come with excellence of speech or of wisdom declaring to you the testimony of God. For I determined not to know anything among you except Jesus Christ and Him crucified. I was with you in weakness, in fear, and in much trembling. And my speech and my preaching were not with persuasive words of human wisdom, but in demonstration of the Spirit and of power, that your faith should not be in the wisdom of men but in the power of God" (1 Corinthians 2:1-5).

This book is intended to increase your knowledge in the basic things of Christ and to encourage a lifetime relationship with your Lord and Savior. Jesus is your breakthrough.

It's simple. Place your faith in what was accomplished at Calvary's cross, surrender your will, and have a relationship with your Savior.

2

SURRENDER

And He died for all, that those who live
should live no longer for themselves, but for
Him who died for them and rose again.

—2 Corinthians 5:15

What does it mean to be a Christian? The dictionary defines a Christian as someone who confesses belief in the teachings of Christ. But the Bible says that even the devil believes—and he's headed for eternal damnation. The Bible is the ultimate authority, not the dictionary.

If you believe in Christ, the world considers you a Christian, but the term was first used in the Bible to describe the disciples in the city of Antioch. Are you living like Jesus' disciples? Don't just say you're a Christian; be a Christian. Going to church isn't enough. The Bible tells us this about Christ's expectation for us: "He died for all, that those who live should live no longer for themselves, but for Him who died for them and rose again" (2 Corinthians 5:15). People used to say they live for the Lord, and we still should. But don't just speak those words; really live for Him.

Have you believed in Him and repented of your sins? Speaking the salvation prayer accomplishes nothing unless you truly believe it. It's nothing more than words unless you believe it. "Without faith it is impossible to please Him, for he who comes to God must believe that He is, and that He is a rewarder of those who diligently seek Him" (Hebrews 11:6). Believe in Him, and believe that what He did was enough to wash away your sins. "For with the heart one believes

"Believe in Him, and believe that what He did was enough to wash away your sins."

unto righteousness, and with the mouth confession is made unto salvation" (Romans 10:10).

If you're in doubt about your salvation, say the following prayer aloud, and truly believe it:

Heavenly Father,

Come into my life. I ask for Your will to be done, and I acknowledge that I am not mine, but Yours. I'm sorry for all the times I've messed up, and I ask for forgiveness of my sins. Let Your blood cleanse me of all unrighteousness. Thank You for a new beginning.

I ask all this in Jesus' name, Amen.

From the moment of salvation, the Holy Spirit begins to do a work in your life, but you must surrender your will to Him. Jesus always did the Father's will; by contrast, Satan put his own will above that of God. Whose future would you prefer—that of Jesus or that of Satan?

When God created all things, He gave man a free will; otherwise there would never have been sin. God isn't going to force you to serve Him. You must willingly choose to submit to God. To live an ungodly life

"You must willingly choose to submit to God."

is to live outside His will. Continue to ask that His will be done in your life, and acknowledge that you are not your own, but you belong to Him. Don't choose to remain empty by refusing to surrender all.

Have you ever wanted something so bad you couldn't stand it? Something you're sure is perfect for you, something that will enrich your life like nothing else ever has, something that so obviously belongs in your life. It's your heart's desire. Now imagine God tells you that this thing you desire is not for you. He doesn't give you an explanation, but He's clear: *It's not for you.* And yet it's what you've always wanted. You've imagined it thousands of times, you've dreamed about it. You just know that it's the best possible thing for you. But His voice still burns in your chest: *It's not for you.* What do you do?

You put God's will above your own. It may hurt for a little while, but trust in Him with your whole heart, and trust in His timing. Put your faith in Him. Sometimes it's not for us to know the why or how. Not every situation will be that hard, but understand that you are His and that He knows your needs. He knows every possible outcome of every situation you'll ever encounter, and He's got you.

You must be willing to let go of anything or any relationship that the Lord wouldn't approve of. If in doubt, go to Him in prayer and ask if it's something you should let go. If you need to ask, chances are He's already convicting you about it. You can't maintain the same lifestyle you had before conversion; your thoughts and desires will change. In order to walk in God's blessings, He has to increase, and you have to decrease. Your spiritual life cannot remain stagnant. You need more of His thoughts and desires, and less of yours. Let Him reveal to you what really matters. Many of the things you think you loved will lose their spark.

We cannot give anything or anyone God's rightful place, including ourselves. John the Baptist said this about Jesus: "He must increase, but I must decrease. He who comes from above is above all; he who is of the earth is earthly and speaks of the earth. He who comes from heaven is above all" (John 3:30-31).

In ancient times, idolatry included the worship of golden figures and statues, but idolatry today can be something as common as the love of money. When we put our faith in the dollar, we're putting money in God's rightful place. Money and possessions are fleeting; store up your riches instead in the kingdom of God.

Remember the example of Moses. He gave up a life of royalty, indulgence, self, and sin to be with the people of God instead, knowing that it wouldn't be easy

"Let Him reveal to you what really matters."

and there'd be suffering. He sacrificed his former life as a child of an earthly king in order to become a child of the one true King, the Almighty God. He knew God's riches were greater than all the riches in Egypt.

Tomorrow you could lose everything you own, but if you've got God, you're better off than the wealthiest man in the world who doesn't have Him.

Athletes, celebrities, politicians, and even preachers are idolized throughout this world, but they're only human. After Adam sinned, everyone (except Jesus) has been born with the same sin nature. No man belongs on a pedestal, not even our spouses or children.

To know God is to know love. Without God, we cannot know true love. Because of Him, we're able to truly love others, but our love for others cannot come before our love for Christ. He must be the love of your life.

To truly surrender all, you mustn't put anything before Him. Self, family, careers, hobbies, finances, or any other earthly pursuit cannot take God's rightful place in your life. He must be above all things. He has plans for His children, and He wants to use you to carry out His will. No earthly accomplishment can compare to fulfilling the will of God. "As it is written:

"Without God, we cannot know true love."

'Eye has not seen, nor ear heard, nor have entered into the heart of man the things which God has prepared for those who love Him'" (1 Corinthians 2:9).

This world can be distracting, and busyness can take hold. Between the requirements of life and the things we voluntarily take on, our lives can be over-whelming. But we must prioritize and put Him first. Sometimes the things that distract us from pursuing the things of God aren't necessarily sinful, but they're keeping us from doing God's will. We all have life requirements and things that must be done, but busy-ness can hinder our Christian walk. Don't be selfish with your time. Satan wants you to be selfish. He wants to puff you up and fill you with pride. He wants you to sit on God's rightful throne, because he knows your temporary reign ends in eternal separation from Christ. God's will for us is that we devote our lives to Him.

Jesus is always available; make yourself available to Him. If something's preventing you from doing what God is calling you to do, you need to reevaluate your priorities. "Do not love the world or the things in the world. If anyone loves the world, the love of the Father is not in him. For all that is in the world—the lust of the flesh, the lust of the eyes, and the pride of life—is not of the Father but is of the world. And the world is passing away, and the lust of it; but he who does the will of God abides forever" (1 John 2:15-17).

He knows your name and the number of hairs on your head. His wants and His desires for you will fulfill you more than anything you could ever dream of or achieve without Him.

Our expectations of God are actually limitations. There's nothing He can't do. The Holy Spirit will lead, guide, and direct your path, but you have to let Him. "Trust in the Lord with all your heart, and lean not on your own understanding; In all your ways acknowledge Him, and He shall direct your paths" (Proverbs 3:5-6). He's already your Savior; it's time to make Him your Lord. Live for Him.

3
RELATIONSHIP

Behold, I stand at the door and knock. If anyone
hears My voice and opens the door, I will come
into him and dine with him, and he with Me.

—Revelation 3:20

A meaningful relationship thrives on effort and commitment, and a relationship with God is no different. A relationship with Him requires reading His Word and talking to Him. Don't put it off; commit to prayer, and meditate on His Word. His Word and His Spirit reveal who He is and what He wants for you. If you want answers, and you want to know what God has for you, get out your Bible.

Before you begin, pray that He speaks to you through it. Pray for clarity and revelation. Put aside earthly knowledge and understanding. Follow Paul's example: "For I determined not to know anything among you except Jesus Christ and Him crucified" (1 Corinthians 2:2).

Begin by reading the first four books of the New Testament: Matthew, Mark, Luke, and John. Then see where the Lord takes you from there. These four Gospels chronicle Jesus' ministry on earth, and they'll undoubtedly make you fall more in love with Him. When we truly love someone, we want to spend time with them. As Jesus said, "Blessed (happy and to be envied)…are those who hear the Word of God and obey and practice it!" (Luke 11:28 AMPC).

Every resource imaginable for studying the Word of God is available to us today. There are multiple

"A meaningful relationship thrives on effort and commitment, and a relationship with God is no different."

Scripture versions (though not all are recommended), study Bibles, concordances, Bible journals, and vast internet resources. There's no excuse not to get to know your Creator. Time is from God, and you wouldn't have the gift of time without Him. Give some back to Him.

Don't restrict God to church services; fellowship with Him in private. Continually push further into the things of Christ. "Set your mind on things above, not on things on the earth" (Colossians 3:2). Pray that His will is done in your life. Pray that He opens doors He wants open, and that He closes doors He wants shut. Pray that He puts relationships in your life that need to be there, and that He removes relationships that don't. While you're praying, pray for the body of Christ, your community, your leaders, and whoever else He brings to mind. Our world is lost, and prayers of the righteous are constantly needed.

The deeper you dig into the Word of God, the more He'll reveal to you. Think of a teacher on the first day of class. He's going to teach his students the basics because they aren't yet ready for greater things he has for them. As they learn, he'll teach them more advanced material. God is the same way. He isn't

"The deeper you dig into the Word of God, the more He'll reveal to you."

going to reveal everything to you at once. The more you mature spiritually, the more He'll illuminate to you. As Paul says, "Physical training is of some value (useful for a little), but godliness (spiritual training) is useful and of value in everything and in every way, for it holds promise for the present life and also for the life which is to come" (1 Timothy 4:8 ampc).

We achieve new levels in our relationship with Christ through prayer and knowledge of His Word, and the closer you get to God, the clearer everything looks. We mustn't be spiritually blind. Before you open His Word, if you're unsure what to pray, pray this prayer:

Heavenly Father,

Thank You for Your Word. I yield my spirit to Yours. Open my eyes and heart to receive from Scripture what You have for me. Speak to my heart as I dig deeper into the things of You. Show me what You want me to see. I ask for a supernatural understanding and discernment of Your Word.

In Jesus' holy name, amen.

Take time out of your day or night and study the Word of God. Get up early or stay up late to meditate on it and to fellowship with Him in prayer. Don't just read chapters to feel you've accomplished something; actually study what you see on those pages. Get to know Him. When your heart is ready to receive, He'll speak to you. An atheist can read the Bible word for word, but unless His heart is earnestly seeking God, he'll profit nothing from it. Don't expect to hear from God with your ears; it's unlikely an audible voice. The Lord will light a fire inside you and you'll feel it in your spirit. The more you get to know Him, the easier it will be to discern His voice from your own.

Worship isn't limited to songs on Sundays; live a life of worship. Sing songs of praise throughout the week. Raise your hands in surrender during prayer in your living room. If you're down to only one shoe, thank Him for it. Praise Him even when He shuts a door that you wanted open. We brought nothing into this world; everything we have is His. It's His very breath in our lungs. "Rejoice always, pray without ceasing, in everything give thanks; for this is the will of God in Christ Jesus for you" (1 Thessalonians 5:16-18).

There's power in the name of Jesus and in the words you speak. Worship Him with your words. Speak life.

"Therefore by Him let us continually offer the sacrifice of praise to God, that is, the fruit of our lips, giving thanks to His name" (Hebrews 13:15). Get into the habit of thanking Him throughout your day. Glorify His name! Worship Him with your actions by obeying His Word and pursuing holiness. "And whatever you do in word or deed, do all in the name of the Lord Jesus, giving thanks to God the Father through Him" (Colossians 3:17).

We serve a most merciful, loving God. Come to Him with a spirit of thanksgiving and a heart of worship. Thank Him regularly for the blessings in your life. Don't take credit for the blessings, and don't give credit where it isn't due. Though God can use a job, a business, or a family member to bless you, ultimately every blessing comes from above.

Pray without ceasing; ask and keep asking; knock and keep knocking. It's easy to turn to Him when we're facing something big, and easy to forget when it's something small. Go to Him with the little things too. Jesus knows your needs more than you do. Pursue the things of God. Include Him, and you'll have His peace in your decisions.

Anyone who has felt the Lord's presence will tell you that there's no peace like the Lord's peace. If you're feeling troubled, go to Him. "Be anxious for nothing, but in everything by prayer and supplication, with thanksgiving, let your requests be made known to God; and the peace of God, which surpasses all understanding, will guard your hearts and minds through Christ Jesus" (Philippians 4:6-7). Lift your hands in surrender, and just talk to Him.

Don't be intimidated by the altar at church. Boldly step into His presence with a repentant heart and lay your problems at His feet. Only in His name is there everlasting peace, everlasting joy, and everlasting hope. Ask Him to give you those things and to move in your life. No drug, food, meditation, therapy, leisure, experience, or anything else can compare to the Lord's presence. The most peace you'll ever experience is found only in Him. As Jesus said, "Peace I leave with you, My peace I give to you; not as the world gives do I give to you. Let not your heart be troubled, neither let it be afraid" (John 14:27). "These things I have spoken to you, that in Me you may have peace. In the world you will have tribulation; but be of good cheer, I have overcome the world" (John 16:33).

The Lord can equip you with supernatural joy when you need it. Ask Him for it. "A merry heart does good, like medicine, but a broken spirit dries the bones" (Proverbs 17:22). The God who made the universe lives in you; trust that He'll never leave you nor forsake you. When your child has a need, you meet it; how much more will your heavenly Father meet your needs!

Joy comes from the Lord, not from circumstances. Temporary happiness can come from our loved ones, possessions, or experiences, but once the high is over, so is the happiness. Then you're stuck trying to fill your life with the next thrill. But God can fill you up with a joy that lasts. It's a joy that can get you through all the in-between times, a joy that's irreplaceable. Some of the wealthiest people are the most miserable and have even ended their own life because they were looking for fulfillment in all the wrong places. They had access to every earthly treasure imaginable—but such things are never enough. Don't seek fulfillment anywhere but with your Savior. Adam and Eve walked with God in the garden. God called Abraham His friend. Nothing else can complete you when you were designed to fellowship with your Creator. True joy can come only from the Holy Spirit. Joy is strength.

When you have no choice other than to rely on God, your relationship with Him is strengthened. Give your problems to Him, and trust that He'll take care of them.

*"Joy comes from the Lord,
not from circumstances."*

You aren't designed to do the heavy lifting. You must decrease, and He must increase. You must fully depend on Him. That doesn't mean you throw your hands up and ignore the situation; it means you trust in Him to take care of the problem, and you rely on His guidance to help you overcome it. When praying, tell Him that you give this situation to Him, because you can't do it on your own. Tell Him that it's not for you to know the why or how, but that you trust Him to take care of it. Stop imagining every possible scenario, and let Him give you the answers. If you give Him your problems, He'll give you your solution.

We're blessed beyond measure, but we will face trials. In the Old Testament, the man Joseph went through a multitude of hardships, but they led him to where God wanted him. He was sold into slavery by his own brothers and later imprisoned, but eventually he became a great leader who blessed God's people immensely. If he hadn't endured all that, he wouldn't have been used by God the way he was.

Thank Him through your trial! We don't always understand why we're facing something, but it could be for our future benefit or for the benefit of another believer. John, one of Jesus' disciples, was exiled on a remote island, but he wrote the book of Revelation during that time. Countless believers have benefited from his trial.

In our trials, Jesus sees a greater need in our lives than what we're focused on. Your burden could be a potential blessing.

A valley, as you know, is a low point surrounded by high points—hills or mountains. Life's trials are the valleys. Your path forward may seem foggy and unclear when you're in the valley, but you're surrounded by mountains. God will help you climb your way out. Self-pity and dwelling on your problems is choosing to stay in the valley. When you're down, the only place left to go is up. Don't let discouragement keep you where you are. Trust that He'll help you climb out of it. "Fear not, for I am with you; be not dismayed, for I am your God. I will strengthen you, yes, I will help you, I will uphold you with My righteous right hand" (Isaiah 41:10).

It's impossible to triumph without a trial, or else what would you have to overcome? How is victory obtained? You must first fight a battle.

We must walk in victory, not defeat. Why would people want to know Jesus if they see Christians walking and talking in misery all the time? Christ took every tragedy we could endure and defeated it. Our victory is in Him. You're on the winning team. You're on the right side, no matter what. God always comes out victorious. If your hope is in Him, you'll never lose it. "And we know that all things work together for good to those who love God, to those who are the called according to His purpose" (Romans 8:28).

Seek the Lord's guidance above all. Go to Him before you make decisions, not just when you need Him to solve the problems caused by your mistakes. Pray that He leads, guides, and directs you in all things.

Get to know God. Every person you know will in some way let you down, but Jesus will never let you down. Seek Him first and surround yourself with godly counsel. Don't allow worldly influence in your life. Your relationship with your Creator is the most important relationship you'll ever have.

4

RIGHTEOUSNESS

All Scripture is given by inspiration of God,
and is profitable for doctrine, for reproof, for
correction, for instruction in righteousness,
that the man of God may be complete,
thoroughly equipped for every good work.

—2 Timothy 3:16-17

L isten to Paul's explanation of how Christ brings us the gift of righteousness: "Therefore, as through one man's offense judgment came to all men, resulting in condemnation, even so through one Man's righteous act the free gift came to all men, resulting in justification of life. For as by one man's disobedience many were made sinners, so also by one Man's obedience many will be made righteous. Moreover the law entered that the offense might abound. But where sin abounded, grace abounded much more, so that as sin reigned in death, even so grace might reign through righteousness to eternal life through Jesus Christ our Lord" (Romans 5:18-21).

We all know someone who has a beautiful family and a successful career. She's always on time and does everything with a smile on her face. Her life appears to embody perfection. You may feel like you'll never measure up. But don't wait to be perfect to live a Christian life, because it will never happen. No matter how great things appear, that person who seems to have it all actually has nothing if she doesn't know Jesus. She's no more righteous than a drug addict or a murderer if she depends on herself to be good enough.

Faith in ourselves and our ability to achieve righteousness always leads to failure. It's impossible to have your own righteousness. It doesn't exist. As Paul said, "I know that nothing good dwells within me, that is, in my flesh. I can will what is right, but I cannot perform it. [I have the intention and urge to do what is right, but no power to carry it out]" (Romans 7:18 AMPC).

Don't measure your success according to man; measure it according to God. There are godly men and women who are wonderful examples of what Christ can do in your life, but there's no perfect person. Even the most admirable man of God messes up. That's why Calvary's cross is our only way out of sin's condemnation. That's why the law failed; people were unable to keep it. Jesus came and fulfilled the law as the only Man without sin.

Don't make it your goal to be like another person. We can admire qualities in others, but understand that we're all unique. Our identity must be in Christ alone. Conform to the image of Christ.

So many in the church today (and outside it) feel that they'll never be good enough in God's eyes because they don't have a full understanding of what Jesus accomplished. No matter how many charitable deeds or good works you do, you can't earn righteousness. We all fall short. Jesus served others, and we can be a blessing to others when we serve them, but so

"Don't measure your success according to man; measure it according to God."

many do it for the wrong reasons. You'll never be righteous from what you give or what you do. The most meaningful thing you can do for someone is to know who Christ is and share Him with them.

We must understand that righteousness is a free gift paid for at the cross. Through faith in Him, we have Christ's righteousness, just as Paul testifies of his aim to "be found in Him, not having my own righteousness, which is from the law, but that which is through faith in Christ, the righteousness which is from God by faith" (Philippians 3:9).

You can have Christ's righteousness, but you must *believe* you have it. Believe that what He did was enough. "For He [God] made Him who knew no sin [His Son Jesus] to be sin for us, that we might become the righteousness of God in Him" (2 Corinthians 5:21).

No one can say you aren't good enough, because you have Christ's righteousness. The most privileged and "churchiest" person cannot come close to the righteousness of God if they don't have Him. No matter where you've been or what you've done, you're good enough. "Through Him [Christ] everyone who believes [who acknowledges Jesus as his Savior and devotes himself to Him] is absolved (cleared and freed) from every charge from which he could not be justified

"*The most meaningful thing you can do for someone is to know who Christ is and share Him with them.*"

and freed by the Law of Moses and given right standing with God" (Acts 13:39 AMPC).

Know who you are. You're a child of God. You have Christ's righteousness because He gave it to you. You just have to believe! Don't make things harder on yourself. Stop trying to be good enough; instead, believe that you are already righteous in God's sight because of what Christ did. See yourself as God sees you. Because you're born again in Christ, you're more than enough. Live like you're loved by the living God.

Satan will try to bring up shameful things from your past. He'll plant thoughts reminding you of what you've done. Satan plants doubt. He'll make you feel unworthy and inferior. He's a liar and wants to prevent you from carrying out God's will. Don't let him hinder you. He tried to plant doubt in Jesus by questioning if He really was the Son of God; how much more will he try to plant doubt in you?

When doubt creeps in, cling to what Jesus accomplished. Don't dwell on what God could have done in your life back then; look at what He *is* doing now, and will *continue* to do in the future.

God knows where you are, where you've been, and where you're going. Scripture says we can do all things through Him who gives us strength. Pray for a double portion of His strength, and believe you've received it—but acknowledge that it's *His* strength. Any good within you is from Him.

In the apostle Paul's letters to the early churches, he didn't speak of his own greatness; instead he spoke of being nothing without Christ. Humble yourself before the Lord. We're nothing without Him. He's our Creator, our heavenly Father, and He deserves the glory for every good and perfect work done through us. As David said about the Lord, "He restores my soul; He leads me in the paths of righteousness for His name's sake" (Psalm 23:3). We have reflective light; it's *His* light, not ours. Give Him credit.

God is the head of the church, and we are the body. He made us in His image, but He made us to be unique individuals. No two people have the same fingerprint. Each individual member of the body of Christ has their own strengths and functions. Though we may not naturally excel at something, God can give us supernatural ability when needed. You'll become who He wants you to be, but you must believe that what He did was enough. There's victory in believing what He did was enough.

5
FREEDOM

Stand fast therefore in the liberty by which
Christ has made us free, and do not be
entangled again with a yoke of bondage.

—Galatians 5:1

Jesus' death on the cross is the atonement for sin, and with it comes sanctification. Sanctification is freedom from sin. Sin is the easiest thing for us, but with the power of the Holy Spirit, we can break free from it. We're no longer slaves to our carnal nature; sin no longer has power over us. No addiction is more powerful than the power of the Holy Spirit. The same God who created the universe lives in you; don't minimize His capabilities.

As much as the world wants to blame sinful behavior on environmental factors or circumstances, the truth is that we're all born into sin, and no good dwells within us. Man isn't born good and then becomes bad; the exact opposite is true. Cain was a member of the first family and was prideful and jealous, and he murdered his own brother. Everyone born into sin is capable of any sin imaginable. Without rebirth in Christ, we aren't worthy to inherit the kingdom of God.

Sin is birthed in the mind, but by conquering your thoughts through faith in His finished work, you can defeat the sin nature within. The mind's vulnerability means we must be Spirit-led. Don't be led by your body and mind, but be led by the Spirit of the living God who dwells within you. Picking up your cross

"The same God who created the universe lives in you; don't minimize His capabilities."

means denying yourself the sinful desires that come so naturally. Remember what Jesus said: "If anyone desires to come after Me, let him deny himself, and take up his cross, and follow Me" (Matthew 16:24).

You don't have to live in bondage to sin. You'll never be put through more temptation than you can handle. "No temptation has overtaken you except such as is common to man; but God is faithful, who will not allow you to be tempted beyond what you are able, but with the temptation will also make the way of escape, that you may be able to bear it" (1 Corinthians 10:13). He'll make a way for you to escape any temptation, but you must believe that He will!

We must have an unshakable faith in Him. Let Him do the doing; you just do the believing! Don't allow your physical senses to control you. There's no sin or temptation placed in front of you that can't be turned away with the power of Christ. It's easy to give in to your feelings, but your first instinct is usually your flesh. If you give in to your every impulse, you put the sinful nature within you above God's plan for your life.

With Jesus, anything is possible. Regardless of what the media, doctors, or well-meaning people say, your God can do all things. There isn't a single situation that He can't pull you out of. There isn't a single addiction

"We must have an unshakable faith in Him."

that He can't deliver you from. The Bible doesn't say He's capable of everything except that. There are no exceptions! As Jesus said, "The things which are impossible with men are possible with God" (Luke 18:27).

The Holy Spirit cannot dwell where a lifestyle of continuous sin resides. Changed behavior is the product of true repentance. There are things in your life that you know God wouldn't approve of. Why hold on to a temporary pleasure that you'll have to answer for? This life is short, but eternity is long. Let the sinful pleasure go. Repent and believe. Remember the Lord's words: "I, even I, am He who blots out your transgressions for My own sake; and I will not remember your sins" (Isaiah 43:25).

It's not that we won't mess up and make a mistake, but we can't hold onto those mistakes, being unwilling to give them up. Repentance is asking for forgiveness of our sin, then giving up that sin. "Therefore, since Christ suffered for us in the flesh, arm yourselves also with the same mind, for he who has suffered in the flesh has ceased from sin, that he no longer should live the rest of his time in the flesh for the lusts of men, but for the will of God" (1 Peter 4:1-2).

We can overcome the flesh only by believing that Christ's finished work was enough. His strength is sufficient in our weakness. When we tackle something that's naturally hard for us, He is glorified when we overcome it through Him. Scripture says that in our weakness, He is strong.

Your past sin does not define you, and your disposition before you found Christ doesn't determine who you'll become after finding Him. When we surrender our will to Him, He cleans house inside us through the presence of His Holy Spirit, and our new self replaces our old self. We're therefore commanded, "Be constantly renewed in the spirit of your mind [having a fresh mental and spiritual attitude], and put on the new nature (the regenerate self) created in God's image, [Godlike] in true righteousness and holiness" (Ephesians 4:23-24 AMPC). Forget your shortcomings according to man, because the new man is daily renewing his mind and conforming to the mind of Christ! "I can do all things through Christ who strengthens me" (Philippians 4:13). He'll make you everything that you're not without Him, if you put His will above your own.

When you eliminate Jesus and rely on man's knowledge to fix your issues, it's only a temporary fix. Your problems will return, possibly worse than before. Jesus is the only eternal solution. You're complete in Him!

You're more than the life you once lived. Jesus gave His life so that you could live eternally. You're invaluable; know your worth. Stop seeking acceptance and validation anywhere but in Him. His opinion of you exceeds all others. He sticks closer than a brother. He's your Advocate before the Father. He has your back and will never leave you. Your closest earthly bond with someone doesn't compare to the bond you have with Him. It will never be broken. He created you. He sacrificed everything for you.

A woman with a sinful reputation washed Jesus' feet and was used by God. We're still hearing of her story two thousand years later. Jesus said, "Her sins, which are many, are forgiven, for she loved much. But to whom little is forgiven, the same loves little" (Luke 7:47). Sometimes those who've run the farthest from God will appreciate His redemption more than others. Imagine someone born into a Christian home who stayed in church and lived what seemed a picture-perfect existence. God was always readily available, so He was often overlooked. She never felt she had to seek Him, so she never experienced His fullness. Now imagine a woman born into a Christian home who backslid with a vengeance. She lived a life of indulgence, vice, sin, and self. She was worldly and experienced a life

*"His opinion of you
exceeds all others."*

without God. When she returned to Him, her passion for her Redeemer couldn't be contained. He had pulled her out of the miry clay. He had rescued her soul. She understood His love because He'd forgiven her. She knows she's nothing without Him. She now has the fullness of God, because she sought it.

We're the body of Christ, and He is the head. We should be in unity with Him. Overcome your sinful nature through faith in His finished work, and you can have the mind of Christ. Ask for His help, and believe that you've received it. There's nothing you can't accomplish, if it aligns with His will. Choose to have the mind of Christ, knowing this truth: "Now the Lord is the Spirit; and where the Spirit of the Lord is, there is liberty. But we all, with unveiled face, beholding as in a mirror the glory of the Lord, are being transformed into the same image from glory to glory, just as by the Spirit of the Lord" (2 Corinthians 3:17-18).

6
REPRESENTATIVES OF HIM

He who says he abides in Him ought
himself to walk just as He walked.

—1 John 2:6

The Christian walk can seem impossible in today's world. We're only a touchscreen away from every possible temptation. Jesus is an afterthought, and sin is encouraged. What has always been good is now bad, and what has always been bad is now good. The Bible has ceased to be the ultimate authority, and the effect has been catastrophic.

The Lord's discernment has never been needed more. We can't pick and choose what is sin and what is not. God is the same today as He was two thousand years ago when Jesus walked the earth. He's the same God who created Adam. Earnestly seek His wisdom, knowledge, and discernment. Nothing the world offers could profit you more.

We represent Christ Jesus, and we must be careful of who and what we endorse. We're His representatives on earth! Our actions should be pleasing to Him. Everywhere you go, you represent Him and His church. The church is not a building but the body of believers. You should honor Him in the things you do, say, read, watch, wear, and listen to. "For the grace of God that brings salvation has appeared to all men, teaching us that, denying ungodliness and worldly lusts, we should live soberly, righteously, and godly in the present age" (Titus 2:11-12). You're a temple of the living God;

> *"We represent Christ Jesus, and we must be careful of who and what we endorse."*

you're not yours, but His. Act like it. Be the light in others' lives. Become a living testimony for what Christ can do. Consider your actions, and choose your words wisely. Don't cause those new in Christ to stumble by behaving like you did before you found Him.

Don't partake in things you know He wouldn't approve of. If God opposes it, you should oppose it. Don't be involved in the darkness of this world, and don't allow it to enter your home. Jesus said, "I have come as a light into the world, that whoever believes in Me should not abide in darkness" (John 12:46). Surround yourself with men and women of God, and ask the Lord to increase the godly relationships in your life.

Everyone needs Jesus, even children. Children have a greater capacity for understanding the things of God than they're given credit for. Plant spiritual seeds in your children from the moment they're born, and encourage a relationship with Jesus. Sunday school and children's church can be a good thing, but the responsibility is with the parents to provide children with the proper foundation. They should see you praying and reading God's Word. If you don't have children, lift up the youth of our world in prayer, because they need it. Pray that they have an experience with the Lord at an early age. Pray for God to use them mightily. Pray that He puts godly relationships into their lives. Satan is out to steal, kill, and destroy, and children are a prime target. They need a relationship with Christ from an early age, but that's a decision they must make for themselves. You can encourage it and give them the proper foundation, but it's up to them to seek Him. We must do our job to equip the youth of today with a true knowledge of Christ. We must teach them how to be true Christians, because the world will teach them just the opposite at every opportunity.

We're being desensitized to sin daily. Christians have taken a step back and allowed sinful ways to enter their minds and their homes. We will answer for what we allow. It's much easier to tolerate secular ways than to oppose them, but we must stand strong. As Jesus said, "Enter by the narrow gate; for wide is the gate and broad is the way that leads to destruction, and there are many who go in by it. Because narrow is the gate and difficult is the way which leads to life, and there are few who find it" (Matthew 7:13-14).

Fall in love with Jesus, not Christianity. Some within the church have made church their God, not Jesus. They give credit to the church for the change in them. Others have hands laid on them in prayer, and they give credit to man for their healings. We are His instrument, but every healing comes from above. Jesus could walk into the

"We must do our job to equip the youth of today with a true knowledge of Christ."

room and they wouldn't recognize Him, because they've idolized the church rather than worshiping Jesus. They put their faith in everything and everyone but Jesus. Don't let anything consume you. If it hinders you from drawing closer to Him, then it's not of God. Programs, activities, and church life can be a blessing, but this cannot come before our love for Christ and carrying out His will.

Times and trends change, but God remains the same. Christian culture is becoming more worldly by the minute. Don't endorse people or things that Jesus Himself wouldn't approve of. "For the time will come when they will not endure sound doctrine, but according to their own desires, because they have itching ears, they will heap up for themselves teachers; and they will turn their ears away from the truth, and be turned aside to fables" (2 Timothy 4:3-4). We must be Spirit-led and seek the Lord's discernment to avoid the pitfalls of false teachings.

"And do not be conformed to this world, but be transformed by the renewing of your mind, that you may prove what is that good and acceptable and perfect will of God" (Romans 12:2). You're a citizen of the kingdom of God. When you walk into a room, before you've said a word, people should be able to tell you're a Christian. People will notice the change in you; let them know where it came from. "Let your light so

"You're a citizen of the kingdom of God."

shine before men, that they may see your good works and glorify your Father in heaven" (Matthew 5:16).

Reject things that represent this world; don't try to blend in with them. We may think we have to sell out to secular ways to remain relevant in today's world, but that's a lie. "Take no part in and have no fellowship with the fruitless deeds and enterprises of darkness, but instead [let your lives be so in contrast as to] expose and reprove and convict them" (Ephcsians 5:11 AMPC). The Word of God will always be the most relevant thing for yesterday, today, and tomorrow. Popularity and "likes" aren't worth the cost of straying from the truth. "Jesus Christ is the same yesterday, today, and forever. Do not be carried about with various and strange doctrines. For it is good that the heart be established by grace" (Hebrews 13:8-9).

The world is saturated with false religions and heresies. Why read books written by man and overlook what was written by man's Creator? The men used to write the books of the Bible were inspired by the Holy Spirit. They were the Lord's instrument, but it's His Word in those pages. Turn away from man-made philosophies disguised within Christian culture. Anything that eliminates Jesus Christ and Him crucified from the equation does not honor God.

"Turn away from man-made philosophies disguised within Christian culture."

Don't compromise. Remember that His Word and Spirit are the ultimate authority. "Beware lest anyone cheat you through philosophy and empty deceit, according to the tradition of men, according to the basic principles of the world, and not according to Christ. For in Him dwells all the fullness of the Godhead bodily; and you are complete in Him, who is the head of all principality and power" (Colossians 2:8-10).

The gospel of Christ is simple, not complicated. Man has overanalyzed, added to, and taken away from His Word, and the result is a divided church. Without the Holy Spirit, we cannot rightfully divide His Word of truth.

Jesus desires true disciples, not just Christians in name only. We can take back the word "Christian" by knowing, loving, and obeying God.

We're called to carry on Christ's work, not begin a new one. With the power of Christ within us, we'll overcome, and we'll finish the race. "Brethren, I do not count myself to have apprehended; but one thing I do, forgetting those things which are behind and reaching forward to those things which are ahead, I press toward the goal for the prize of the upward call of God in Christ Jesus" (Philippians 3:13-14).

7

THE HOLY SPIRIT AND THE POWER IT CONTAINS

'Not by might nor by power, but by
My Spirit,' says the Lord of hosts.

—Zechariah 4:6

The Holy Spirit is a mystery to some Christians, and that has to change. We live in a world where the Bible is available on our phones, tablets, watches—the list goes on. If there's something you don't understand, don't hesitate to seek God for the answers. Pray for clarity and understanding, and find the answers in His Word. We're so inclined to do a web search and read a blog post, but we refuse to go to the source! Don't be intimidated by the Word of God. If you're hungry, you'll get fed.

When God puts something on your heart, when miracles happen, when He convicts you of something, when you feel the Lord's presence, when an act of God happens, you can credit the Holy Spirit. You feel Him when you hear that one worship song. You feel Him when the preacher preaches on what you've been praying about. You feel Him when you get confirmation of something the Lord put on your heart.

The Holy Spirit is one of three distinct Persons in one God, along with the Father and the Son, Jesus Christ. The Holy Spirit is also called the Holy Ghost. The Holy Spirit resides within the believer at the moment of salvation, but the baptism of the Holy Spirit is a free gift that follows. When John the Baptist baptized Jesus in the Jordan River, the Holy Spirit descended upon Him like a dove, and then His earthly

"Pray for clarity and understanding, and find the answers in His Word."

ministry began. The miracles Jesus did were done by God as a man with the power of the Holy Spirit.

After His resurrection, Jesus didn't just appear and leave. He was on the earth for forty days preaching the kingdom of God. When He went to be with the Father, He gave His disciples directions to stay in Jerusalem, for the Comforter was coming. "And being assembled together with them, He commanded them not to depart from Jerusalem, but to wait for the Promise of the Father, 'which,' He said, 'you have heard from Me; for John truly baptized with water, but you shall be baptized with the Holy Spirit not many days from now'" (Acts 1:4-5). God would not have sent His Holy Spirit if it wasn't in His will for us to have it. Jesus isn't physically here with us, but He has sent His Holy Spirit in His place to be our Comforter, Counselor, Adviser, Consultant, Guide, Mentor, and more. God sent us the only therapist we could ever need, and it's free.

Jesus was very clear about the distinction of the baptism of the Holy Spirit and the indwelling that happens at salvation. When He spoke of the baptism of the Holy Spirit, He had already died and risen again. He had already died for our sins. The believers He spoke to were already saved, making the baptism of the Holy Spirit a separate thing.

Water baptism and baptism of the Holy Spirit are not requirements for eternal life, but the baptism of the Holy Spirit gives the believer power, boldness, and spiritual gifts that cannot be attained otherwise. Confusion regarding the Holy Spirit has divided so many within the church. The church is powerless without the Holy Spirit; that's where the power of God lies! Healings, miracles, and deliverance from demonic oppression happen when the power of God falls upon His people. The Holy Spirit contains the same power that Jesus Himself had. Peter raised Tabitha from the dead through the power of the Holy Spirit and called on a paralytic to walk.

You need the power of God's Holy Spirit. Remember what Jesus told His disciples: "Behold, I send the Promise of My Father upon you; but tarry in the city of Jerusalem until you are endued with power from on high" (Luke 24:49).

On the day of Pentecost, the Holy Spirit fell upon the believers in the upper room, and they received the baptism of the Holy Spirit with the evidence of speaking in tongues. "And they were all filled with the Holy Spirit and began to speak with other tongues, as the Spirit gave them utterance" (Acts 2:4).

Nothing can beat God. If you want His power to help you carry out His will, seek the baptism of the

"You need the power of God's Holy Spirit."

Holy Spirit. If you want supernatural gifts, ask to be filled. The initial baptism and speaking in tongues are the door that leads to the other spiritual gifts. "But the manifestation of the Spirit is given to each one for the profit of all: for to one is given the word of wisdom through the Spirit, to another the word of knowledge through the same Spirit, to another faith by the same Spirit, to another gifts of healings by the same Spirit, to another the working of miracles, to another prophecy, to another discerning of spirits, to another different kinds of tongues, to another the interpretation of tongues. But one and the same Spirit works all these things, distributing to each one individually as He wills" (1 Corinthians 12:7-11). You don't have to be at the altar to be filled; it can happen in your backyard or in your living room. Lift your hands in surrender and worship Him. Don't get impatient if it doesn't happen right away. Persistently seek Him, and believe that it's a free gift, which you'll receive in His perfect timing.

Once filled with the Holy Spirit, you'll feel a fire inside you that you've never felt before. It will empower you and push you further into the things of God. You'll want more of Him. You'll want so much of Him that you can't contain it. Your desire to dive into the things of God will be intensified. You'll have a boldness and strength like never before, and you'll be able to combat whatever Satan tries to throw your way.

When we pray in tongues, we are praying for God's will to be done. Praying in your heavenly language is praying from God, to God. When you don't know what to pray, pray in the Spirit. Your prayers could impact someone you've never even met.

"I still have many things to say to you, but you cannot bear them now. However, when He, the Spirit of truth, has come, He will guide you into all truth; for He will not speak on His own authority, but whatever He hears He will speak; and He will tell you things to come. He will glorify Me, for He will take of what is Mine and declare it to you. All things that the Father has are Mine. Therefore I said that He will take of Mine and declare it to you" (John 16:12-15).

The Holy Spirit is not to be confused with the fruits of the Spirit. An apple tree produces apples, not pears, the same way the born-again believer produces the fruit of the Spirit, not the flesh. A Christian is evidenced by his actions. By their fruits you will know them. "The fruit of the Spirit is love, joy, peace, longsuffering, kindness, goodness, faithfulness, gentleness, self-control. Against such there is no law" (Galatians 5:22-23).

We must be Spirit-led. Christ accomplished what it takes to enable us to overcome the desires of the flesh. You're being conformed to His image daily, and the closer you get to Him, the more conviction you'll face. He doesn't want you to live like you did before. Ask for His strength, and believe you've received it. Believe that what He did was enough. There's victory in believing that what He did was enough.

Remember that unless your faith is in the proper place, you will fail. Someone who isn't Spirit-led is led by their flesh, their sinful carnal nature. "Now the doings (practices) of the flesh are clear (obvious): they are immorality, impurity, indecency, idolatry, sorcery, enmity, strife, jealousy, anger (ill temper), selfishness, divisions (dissensions), party spirit (factions, sects with peculiar opinions, heresies), envy, drunkenness, carousing, and the like. I warn you beforehand, just as I did previously, that those who do such things shall not inherit the kingdom of God" (Galatians 5:19-21 AMPC).

Whoever hates is capable of murder. Whoever lusts is capable of adultery. We were born into sin, but upon accepting Christ we were born again into the kingdom of God. Strive to live a holy life, and put kingdom things first. "Or do you not know that your body is

"Ask for His strength, and believe you've received it."

the temple of the Holy Spirit who is in you, whom you have from God, and you are not your own?" (1 Corinthians 6:19). "[Live] as children of obedience [to God]; do not conform yourselves to the evil desires [that governed you] in your former ignorance [when you did not know the requirements of the Gospel]. But as the One Who called you is holy, you yourselves also be holy in all your conduct and manner of living. For it is written, you shall be holy, for I am holy" (1 Peter 1:14-16 AMPC).

He'll transform you. You just have to place your faith in what was accomplished at Calvary's cross, surrender your will, and have a relationship with Him.

There's no greater tale of redemption and transformation than the story of Saul of Tarsus, who later became the apostle Paul. Saul was a zealot, a Pharisee of Pharisees who intensely persecuted the followers of Jesus. He helped put believers into prison and to death, yet our God would use him as His chosen vessel to carry out His will. God completely altered the course of Saul's life, and his name was changed to Paul. He was a new creation in Christ. Paul wrote thirteen books of the New Testament, preached the gospel of Christ, and played a large part in establishing the early church. He had been a murderer of Christians, but God turned his life around and used him mightily.

Paul was a redeemed man filled with the Holy Spirit. If God can use Paul, He can use you. If you're waiting to be perfect to live for God, don't. Let the Holy Spirit mold you. Become a product of Christ. "Therefore, if anyone is in Christ, he is a new creation; old things have passed away; behold, all things have become new" (2 Corinthians 5:17).

COMMON CHRISTIAN TERMS

Anointing
a special blessing from God

Atonement
God's plan to redeem mankind, accomplished through Christ's ultimate sacrifice

Bible
God's infallible (without error) Word

Born-again
spiritual rebirth in Christ

Born into sin
the sinful nature everyone has been born with since Adam first sinned

Christian
believer, follower of Christ

Church
the body of Christ

Condemned
to be found guilty

Faith
the substance of things hoped for and the evidence of things not seen (see Hebrews 11); a requirement to come before the Lord

Flesh
man's sinful carnal nature

Glorified
exalted

Holy
spiritually pure

Holy Spirit
one of three distinct Persons in one God, along with
the Father and the Son, Jesus Christ; also called the
Holy Ghost

Hypocrite
a fraud; someone who doesn't follow beliefs they
profess (refer to Matthew 23:23-28)

Idolatry
putting something or someone in God's rightful
place

Justification
declaration of innocence, righteousness

Redemption
repurchased and delivered from sin by Christ's
sacrificial blood at the cross

Repentance
to ask forgiveness and give up said sin

Revelation
a supernatural communication from God

Righteousness
morally upstanding; a free gift from God paid for at
Calvary's cross, obtained only through faith in Christ

Salvation
God's plan of redemption from sin; eternal life

Sanctification
freedom from sin; set apart

Sin
to disobey God

Spirit
who you are, your being

Surrender
wholehearted submission to God

Worship
to honor and praise

ABOUT THE AUTHORS

ANNA SCHULTZ has experienced firsthand the life-changing power of a relationship with Christ. From blessed beginnings to a life of rebellion against God, her story has come full circle. She's transforming daily into who He has called her to be. She is a dedicated homeschooler and is involved in youth and worship ministry. Anna lives on a farm in the Midwest with her husband and three children.

HEATHER HENDON was born into a family of ministers and was baptized in the Holy Spirit at eight years old. Despite experiencing God's power early on, she spent years trying to fill her void with everything except God. After years of running, she finally answered His call and is a living testimony of His power. She is involved in several church ministries and writes worship songs. Heather is a grateful wife and mother and lives in the hills of Indiana.